I0532307

I AM
YOU ARE
HE IS
JUST LIKE ME
A MOTHER'S JOURNEY

Patrice Brown

TABLE OF CONTENTS

WHY THIS BOOK? WHY NOW? WHY NOT?

This book is not a book about a child with a special need that can play Mozart, sing melodiously, or recite long lists of important information in minutes. This book is not about a mom who has handled every situation correctly and wants to tell the world how to parent a special needs child the "right" way. This book is not about a family that handled everything perfectly. This book, really, is not about me at all. It is about a child that was labeled as having autism spectrum disorder at two and a half years of age. A child that is a brother to four siblings, went to day care, attended public school, and had only the therapy insurance would cover. It's about his struggles, his triumphs, his failures and how I look back over them and see the hand of God working through him. It's about my son, Marc Brown, whom I love with all my heart. My love that is not dependent on if he can or cannot do or say something "correctly." It's about recognizing that type of love that God has for us. Acknowledging that even if I cannot, God is still able because of that love He has for me.

I have been so hesitant in writing this book. I was fearful because I am opening myself and my family up to others. I am writing only what is truthful to me from my experiences. I do not consider myself a writer or a novelist. I am a

Christian who was a wife at the time of the events, and I am a mother who loves the Lord with all my heart and truly holds fast to my favorite scriptures:

> *"And we know that all things work together for good to them that love God, to them who are the called according to his purpose." – Romans 8:28 NIV*

> *"'For I know the plans I have for you,' declares the Lord, 'plans to prosper you and not to harm you, plans to give you hope and a future.'" – Jeremiah 29:11 NIV*

> *"For the Spirit God gave us does not make us timid, but gives us power, love and self-discipline." – 2 Timothy 1:7 NIV*

> *"Seek the Kingdom of God above all else and live righteously, and he will give you everything you need." – Matt 6:33 NLT*

And my favorite words in the Bible: "It came to pass…"

I do not claim to be an expert at anything. I am just a regular person with gifts and talents given to me by the Lord. When I began writing in 2012, I was a nontraditional student studying Secondary Education - Mathematics, volunteering in a community organization, and an active member of my church. I was 41 years old and lived in a small three-bedroom apartment with my husband and four children. As I complete this book, I am a 50-year-old high school Mathematics teacher and Marc is now 20. He has walked across the stage as a high school graduate. I consider myself an average person who happens to have a child with autism.

Did I get frustrated? Do I still get frustrated? The answer is YES!

Did I ask God why? Did I say "Lord, I can't handle this?" Did I make it about me? Did I blame myself? The answer is YES!

Am I moving forward? Are we moving forward? Am I dealing with it? Is it dealing with me? YES!

Now for the big questions:
Am I growing from the experience? YES
Has it taught me to trust and rely on God? YES
Has the experience increased my faith? YES

There are many speakers and books about children with autism. Many children that I read about are high functioning. These children have the ability to talk and have usually discovered a uniquely brilliant gift or talent God has given them. Marc is not considered to be a child with high functioning autism. There are many support groups for parents of children with autism. But support groups and reading the books did not help me.

There are stages to growth. Some of us skip stages and some of us can sometimes become stuck in a stage of growth and then have a growth spurt. I think the latter was me.

It reminds me of my oldest son, Sean. As he grew, his feet grew. Every year his shoe size increased one whole size. I remember he was in a size 8 shoe for two years. We thought his feet had stopped growing. He had three pairs of shoes, and he was never rough on shoes. My husband and I bought him a pair of size 8 shoes in December. We took him for another pair of shoes in May, he was still a size 8. So, it was confirmed, or so we thought, that his foot had stopped growing. We took him again in August (beginning of school) and he was a size 10 ½. We had some mixed emotions that day! We were surprised, not only at how he had skipped some sizes, but we were more surprised that he had been wearing shoes 2 ½ sizes too small and never said anything. He never complained, he never limped as if his feet were hurting, just never said a word. He said, "well I was uncomfortable, but I didn't want to bother you and dad."

That was me. I was uncomfortable in the groups and reading the books, but I didn't want to be a bother. See, a size 8 may fit some people and that is great. But I was having a growth spurt. I quickly went from the denial, blame, and "woe is me" stage to the "fix it" stage (my size 8). I was in the "fix it" stage because I just knew something was broken. It had to be! I wanted to figure out what was broken in my child, then fix it and move on with life like "normal." I thought in a matter of a few weeks, months, or even a few years, Marc would be alright. The doctors, specialists, therapists, and teachers were going to fix him. What I found out was the size 8 shoes were not my permanent size. I was going to have a growth spurt. I found that Marc was not the one who was broken and who needed to be fixed. God wanted me to be uncomfortable and move up in my size of faith. I needed to add some things quickly in order to move up in sizes.

> *"For this very reason, make every effort to add to your faith goodness; and to goodness, knowledge; and to knowledge, self-control; and to self-control, perseverance; and to perseverance, godliness; and to godliness, mutual affection, and to mutual affection, love."*
> *– 2 Peter 1:5-7 NIV*

This book is not in any chronological order. It is a true collection of lessons and experiences along this mom's journey.

THE BEGINNING

...And it came to pass.

— Luke 2:1a

I remember it as if it were just yesterday, "Yep, Mr. and Mrs. Brown, your son has autism."

It was March 29, 2004. We had only been in the office with Marc and the neurologist for all of ten minutes. There was no table, no examination. Marc looked through toys and played with them in his own special way. He lined them up, categorized, and grouped them. The doctor asked him questions that for any two-year-old, would be a cinch to answer; but of course, Marc did not answer or even acknowledge the doctor was even in the room talking to him. The doctor talked to my husband and me as I looked past him and watched Marc. That was all it took, ten minutes! Ten minutes to diagnose my son with something I knew nothing about and did not even know existed until his pediatrician asked me if I had heard of it before. And that was only a month ago! Ten minutes! To me that ten minutes seemed like 5 seconds in the scope of things.

My response, "Well, Happy Birthday to me! Okay, so how do we fix it? What do we do next? When will he be 'normal' again?"

My husband's response, "Why?

LESSON LEARNED:

At that moment, it became all about me. Our discussion on the way home was us re-evaluating our parenting, our past failures, our lifestyle, anything, and everything we did or did not do. I thought "why Marc?" We had Sean Jr. and autism didn't happen to him. My husband had a daughter, my stepdaughter, and she was fine. Autism didn't happen to her. Was it me? Was it something I did? Was it …? I soothed myself with a thought: we have another appointment at the hospital for a series of tests and they will find out what is wrong and the doctors at the hospital will fix it. It will be fixed.

I made his having autism about me. I learned that this is about my child and God working through him and in him. God had given me the opportunity as a parent to witness His love and to learn to love unconditionally while helping Marc along one of life's many journeys.

WHAT IS NORMAL?

I praise you because I am fearfully and wonderfully made;
your works are wonderful; I know that full well.
– Psalm 139:14

So, I hear people around saying, "My child is not normal, he/she has autism." I have been fighting with the term "normal" for a while now. I have heard teachers say, "So he is beginning to do things just like a normal child." What is a normal child? I have five children and not one does the same thing or acts just like the other, so are they normal or abnormal? They all started walking, talking, writing at different stages in their life. Are they regular or do we put a label on each of them as irregular? How do we determine that and who determines it? Marc is unique just like every other child. He uses his mind and figures things out. Sometimes he needs help, but recently he's been doing well on his own.

It took me a while to realize it, but just as I must learn Spanish to speak to someone whose only language is Spanish, and that person would have to learn English to speak to me, the same concept applies to Marc. I must take the time to learn his language, gestures, and signs as well as he must learn my language, gestures, and signs. It doesn't happen overnight because he and I are both learning a second language. We both must try and add to all the rules and concepts of our first language to truly grasp the second one. So what, someone may not understand him when he speaks or may get a little bothered because he is getting loud as a result of me telling him no, he can't have or do something; let's all remember, he is a child, and we are all in the learning process. If a person only spoke English and they tried to speak to someone who only speaks French, wouldn't they have a hard time? If someone is deaf and they try and sign to someone who does not know sign language, wouldn't they have a hard time?

I am enjoying becoming bilingual. I will be a master on this journey to speaking that language that many Neurologists and Pediatricians call "gibberish." For Marc and I, gibberish will be our normal.

LESSON LEARNED:

I defined Normal and Regular. You too can define Normal and Regular. What is normal is what you have defined as normal. Do not allow others to define normal and regular for you, because that will only frustrate both you and your child. Embrace each other's difference and learn from one another.

HE HAS A VOICE

One day Jesus told his disciples a story to show that they should always pray and never give up.

– Luke 18:1

For Marc, speech therapy started before he was diagnosed with Mild Autism Syndrome Disorder. He had constant ear infections as a baby into his early 2's and was repeatedly given antibiotics to treat them. When we moved to Florida and my husband left the military, Marc's new civilian doctor noticed the number of ear infections and treatments and thought it was odd he had never gone to see a specialist. It was during an ear infection that Marc began his regression in his speech development. He would try and form words, but they were coming out as "gibberish." When we arrived at the specialist's office, we discovered Marc had almost completely lost hearing in one ear as a result of the ear infections he suffered. Because his speech regression and hearing loss occurred simultaneously, Marc's Pediatrician sent him to speech therapy. Marc had surgery to insert tubes in his ears and within six months his hearing was restored; however, his speech was not.

I recall Marc sitting in the highchair in front of the speech pathologist trying his best to form his mouth in the same fashion as hers. He tried so hard, but when the sound came out it was gibberish. There was a disconnect from his brain to his mouth. He wanted so badly to say the same thing, but it was not happening. She then determined that it was going to be "back to the basics" with Marc. No words, just saying the letter and the sound. Marc has since seen different speech therapists in and out of school and they always seem to have to stay on those basics… letter name and letter sound. Marc, although he tried his best, didn't get past this for years.

Then one day, it was as if a lightbulb turned on. Something connected his brain to his mouth, Marc said "dawgu" as a dog stood in front of us.

"Mommy Marc said dog, Marc said dog!" my older son yelled.

"Marc," I said, "What is that?"

Marc looked up at me puzzled and said, "dawgu" as if saying "You don't know mommy?"

"That's right Marc, that's a dog." I said as tears of joy ran down my face.

My son, at the age of six had found his voice. Although this was just the beginning of a new journey for him, it was the end to a very long, tiring, and tedious trip.

LESSON LEARNED:

Never give up. Marc was trying hard, and it was probably more frustrating for him because he heard the therapist and he saw my face and knew what I wanted. He knew what I expected, but he couldn't please me. All he wanted to do was please me. He lived for the smile on my face and the hugs. He wanted the feelings of love that are given when he had accomplished something. I had to make sure that I recognized not just the accomplishments but the attempts as well. We must remember that had it not been for the attempting, there would never be the moment when they accomplish it. Getting something right is big, but attempting time after time, again and again, failure after failure, is BIGGER!! Marc didn't give up, why should I?

FIRST STEPS

Father, if you are willing, take this cup from me; yet not my will,
but yours be done.
— Luke 24:42 NIV

I felt a tug on my pants. "Yes, Marc. What do you want?"

Never a verbal answer, just a little finger pointing in the direction of his desires. When would this end? He received speech therapy at school and personal therapy outside of school three days a week. Was this helping at all? Why wasn't he talking by now? I wanted him to move at my pace, not his pace. I wanted results now, not when he was ready to give them. I wanted… and that was it. I wanted! God did not want what I wanted at that time, and I had to embrace that. I had to conform and work with that.

2007 was the year that Marc was ready. Ready to write, begin using words, and attempt to communicate by means other than his finger pointing and screams of frustration. Marc was 6 and he decided he would say simple words like tiger, cat, dog, go, and horse (his favorite). I remember that sparkle in his eye when we both understood one another, and we would share a smile for his accomplishment. Just thinking of it reminds me that every little thing happens for a reason while on life's journey. Although I wanted so much to believe Marc's inability to talk was all about him, I found out it was teaching me something called patience and unconditional love.

LESSON LEARNED:

Remember, things may not come when we want it. Do not give up and do not feel defeated. There will be a breakthrough after you learn your lesson. Every breakthrough will not look the same, but it will come. We must learn the lessons of patience, love and understanding in a way that we will always remember. We must cherish the small things. Find joy in the little things. Whatever it is, it will come when you and your child are both ready. Sometimes we must change our timeline to God's timeline in order to notice the little things and have more shared smiles of accomplishments.

HIS NAME

A good name is more desirable than great riches; to be esteemed is better than silver or gold.

– Proverbs 22:1

When I think about it, I mean really sit back and think about it, I have concluded that God trusts me. He really trusts little old me. What a revelation! The God that created the heavens and the earth; the God that knows our beginning and our end; the God above all, trusts me! Wow! He gave me one of his precious spirits. One that no one else would or could possibly understand; one that was different than what the world says is "normal." One that stands out from the crowd. One that will test my faith, trust, and belief. One that will make me question how, why, when, and for how long? A spirit enclosed in a body and named Marc.

We named Marc after my husband's younger brother who died at the age of three. His name was Marcus. My husband agreed to shorten the name to Marc because I wanted all of the boys to have 4 letters in their names (just my normal that I talk about later). My husband also picked out his middle name because his middle name had to start with the letter A, my husband's family tradition. I never looked up the meaning of the name Marc before I named him as I did with Sean Jr. I just knew that was going to be his name.

Today, as I write, I decided to research Marc's name. His full name is Marc Antony Brown. The meaning of Marc is "warlike." The meaning of Antony is "worthy of praise, of value." Brown is symbolic of man on earth.

In all, God trusts me with Marc, a male on earth who is valuable and warlike. I then looked up warlike and it read: "fit, qualified and ready for war." Marc is a valuable man who is fit, qualified and ready for war.

My next question was "war with whom or what?" Quickly I thought, "war with me!" Many times, I have felt that we were at war. Me trying to understand him, communicate with him, and change him to be "normal" while he opposed me and fought me all the way.

As Marc grows and develops, I have concluded that we, Marc and I, are not on opposing sides. We are on the same side. We just needed to understand how to communicate with one another. How to appreciate each other's differences and love through it.

So now, we are ready to fight together, and his name tells me that he will be victorious. It's all in a name!

LESSON LEARNED:

What we call our children has a lot to do with what they may achieve and what we believe they can achieve. It is sometimes just understanding who they are and that we are in this together that makes all the difference.

A GLIMPSE INTO
THE FUTURE

*Jesus looked at them and said, "With man this is impossible,
but with God all things are possible."*
– Matthew 19:26 NIV

On the last day of summer camp, Marc walked up to me when he got home. "For you." he said as he handed me the paper lantern he made. I had to fight back the tears. He looked at me and smiled. I did not even notice he had something in his hand. I was amazed at the fact that I clearly understood what he said, and what he said was not something he had said before. This was new. And he knew what the words meant! His actions went with the words coming out of his mouth. He said something without being prompted, without being told exactly what to say and how to say it. Such a little thing was enormous in my eyes. I gave him a hug and he turned and ran away laughing.

Thank You, Lord, for a glimpse at what is to come. It seems every time I think it might not happen; you send me a glimpse of what will be.

LESSON LEARNED:

Remember to have joy in the little things. In the little things we see a glimpse of their future. My Marc will be on his own one day and looking back on these years as the steppingstones to who he has become

SECRET PLACE

Then, because so many people were coming and going that they did not even have a chance to eat, he said to them, "Come with me by yourselves to a quiet place and get some rest."

– Mark 6:31 NIV

"Marc, Marc, MARC!" I would call his name. He would not even look my way.

"Marc, you better answer me!"

Yet still no response. He would not even blink when I called him.

CLAP! I hit my hands together as loud as I could and no response.

Now I'm frustrated. I know my child can hear me. I know that I am yelling. I can't believe he is ignoring me.

I walked over to him. "MARC!" Still no response.

I stood in front of the television. I bent down and looked into his eyes. It's the strangest thing to see, your child looking through you. His eyes were fixed. They did not even move when I got closer to his face.

The questions that would begin to run through my mind: Is he looking at me?

Can he even see me?

Can he see through me?

What does he see?

What is wrong with him?

I then got extremely close to his face and yelled, "MARC!"

He blinked, and his eyes changed. It's not that they

moved or even shifted. They just changed. He stopped looking through me and looked at me. It was as if he just noticed I was in the same room and standing in front of him. He was no longer focused on the world in his head, but he was now focused on me and the world we shared together.

What I just described was a glimpse of the regression we witnessed in Marc at the age of two. This was one of the signs that something was different about him. I remember thinking he was just stubborn. I would clap my hands, yell and scream his name. I would get so frustrated with him for not responding.

At age eleven, had it changed?

Well, he doesn't do it as much. When I see him zoning out, I quickly call his name and get his attention. Sometimes clapping twice helps him come back to our shared world. Other times I just leave him alone. When he goes to his place, his secret place, he is so focused. He is concentrating. When it is time for him to come out of his secret place, he comes to me and gives me the best hugs, looks at television, draws, or begins to organize and line up his toys. But he seems more content and calmer after he leaves his secret place.

Looking back at how I would react when he went to his secret place, I realized I was quick to get frustrated. Not frustrated because Marc would not respond to me, but frustrated because I did not understand. Frustrated because I was not included in his secret place. I was not even invited. It was Marc's place. It was his place where he found peace. He seemed to be content there. So why did I allow that to bother me so much? Why did I turn it into him not obeying or respecting me? Maybe he was obeying and respecting his time with God. Maybe God was showing me that I too needed to find that place. My own secret place. A place where I could hear from Him. A place where I could be at peace. A place where the outside world was dead to me. A place where I could just bask in His presence and not allow the noises of this world to penetrate. A place of contentment and rest.

LESSON LEARNED:

As parents of children with special needs, our desire is that our child will learn something that will help them. We often forget that we have much to learn from them. I would quickly get frustrated and upset because Marc didn't do things like other children. He didn't respond like others. He didn't act like others. But then I was reminded of God's words:

> *But ye are a chosen generation, a royal priesthood, a holy nation, a peculiar people; that ye should shew forth the praises of him who hath called you out of the darkness into his marvelous light.*

> *— 1 Peter 2:9 KJV*

I thank God that my child is different, not like the multitude. I press to learn as much as possible from him. Although I will get frustrated, still question, still react, I will still trust that the Lord my God will use each experience along this journey as a lesson to draw me closer to Him.

TREASURE BOX

But store up for yourselves treasures in heaven, where moths and vermin do not destroy, and where thieves do not break in and steal.
— Matthew 6:30 NIV

The year was 2008, Marc was 7 years old. I remember taking him to a school for children with autism. A friend of mine took her son there and her son could talk, answer questions, and from what I could see, was further along to being "normal" than Marc. Yes, I knew autism was a spectrum. I understood what spectrum meant, but what I did not understand was why my child was still in pull ups and this child, two years younger, was potty trained. Why my child did not hold a conversation, and this child could start conversations. I had to get my child into that school because I just knew it was the school that made the difference between the two.

I remember going to the school and taking a tour. Everything seemed perfect to me. Marc liked the fact that he would see horses from the campus, so he was ready to go. I filled out the paperwork and that day Marc was put on the waiting list.

The school year started, and Marc's name was not up for enrollment yet, so he had to attend a public school close by that had an autism unit. I hated it. It was not the autism school. It was not the place that I thought would help my child the most. I just wanted him out. When I talked about the school Marc was enrolled in, I frowned, and the tone of my voice would change to almost disgust. I let it be known that I did not care for the school. As I reflect, I had no real reason to dislike the school. The teachers there never had a chance. I couldn't even tell you if Marc had any advancements while there because my time was spent on disliking the school. My focus was on getting Marc into the school I thought was right for him, the autism school.

Within the second month of the school year, the autism school had an opening. I was jumping for joy. I could not wait. My child was going to progress and become like every other child in just one year. I just knew it!

After the first few weeks, I noticed some things. There was no communication between me and his teacher. I had no idea what was going on during the day with Marc. I didn't know what he was being taught, how he was responding, if he was having a good or bad day. I immediately called for a conference and asked for a communication book or folder between me and the teacher. The first school was doing this, but I missed it because my focus was on the wrong place.

I then realized Marc never had homework. Why was this? He always had homework before, at the other school. I wrote a note. I was told homework would consist of practicing life skills that were being taught in class. Life skills? What else is being taught in class? I wanted Marc to learn how to talk, count, read, etc. The other school focused on academics, but I did not notice because I was too busy comparing my child to someone else's and thinking he had to be at the same school to achieve the same results.

Within the second semester, I received a letter that Marc's teacher was no longer at the school. She could not handle working with children with autism and went to work at a "regular" school. Marc was now without a permanent teacher and his schedule changed daily. Marc began to regress. The teachers and aides at the other school had been there for over five years. But that was not important to me then because I wanted Marc in the autism school that I thought would fix him.

LESSON LEARNED:

Marc is unique, just as every child is. He will learn differently. He will accomplish different things in his own timing during his life. He is always learning and will always be capable of learning. I must, as a parent, remember that it's about Marc's needs, not my wants. I wanted Marc to talk at that moment; however, Marc needed structure, care, consistency, nurturing, and academics. Is Marc talking now? Yes, in his own unique way. Does he talk as well as others? It really doesn't matter. Marc has grown and developed at his pace and in God's timing.

I have learned to sit back and let the blessings unfold instead of trying to do everything myself at my timing. I see Marc's experiences and his journey as a gift. It reminds me of a big treasure box. I am getting little treasures one at a time. When I get one, I must spend time to open it and play with it for a while. As soon as I decide on a favorite, God gives me a better treasure from inside the box This process keeps repeating over and over again. I have an endless treasure box filled with gifts from God, and his name is Marc.

A MIND OF HIS OWN

Be thankful in all circumstances, for that is God's will for you who belong to Christ Jesus.

– 1 Thessalonians 5:18

One night after dinner, Marc came into my bedroom. I was sitting on the edge of the bed, and he crawled on the bed behind me. He bent over so his lips were almost touching my ear and whispered, "open."

At first, I did not make out what he was saying, so I said, "What is it, Marc?"

Again, he whispered "open."

This time he dangled some cookies over my head. I turned over and said, "No Marc, it's too late. You don't need cookies."

He immediately got up, ran into the kitchen, and put the cookies back on the table. He then returned, laid on the bed beside me and mumbled, "Mommy's mean."

I quickly said, "What did you say?" He looked at me with the cutest smile.

My husband responded, "He said, 'Mommy's mean.'"

"No, he didn't. He can't say that! Or, can he?"

I turned to Marc and said, "Is mommy nice or mean?"

He formed his lips to say mean, but then started making humming noises. All with a smile on his face while looking at me out of the corner of his eye. Okay, I thought, let me put this another way. I just wanted to make sure Marc was understanding what I was saying.

"Marc, is mommy good or bad?"

He looked at me and formed his mouth to say "bad" but did not say it. He laughed and backed away instead.

"See honey, I told you, he said Mommy was mean. He just doesn't want to hurt your feelings."

Hurt my feelings, I thought. Not at all. As a matter of fact, I was so elated about him understanding how and when to use the word mean. What a joy to realize that my baby (okay, he was 10) had a mind of his own and knew how to express his feelings using words.

You see, instead of getting upset about this, I felt at that moment, my child did think I was a mean mommy. He had eaten his dinner, so why couldn't he have a snack? But what we didn't know was God was going to use that moment of being a "mean mommy" as one of his accomplishments on his journey. To hear my child, my child with autism, my 10-year-old that has very limited language skills, my baby boy that has neurologists baffled, tell me, yes tell me how he feels, was the highlight of my day. It just re-affirmed that autism does not have him. He will conquer this and be successful in life.

LESSON LEARNED:

Take joy in the little things. Reward the little things. Smile at the little things. Do not always find fault. Do not be easily offended or you may miss the blessing.

STOP AND GO

Peter said, "Lord, if that is really you, tell me to come to you on the water." Jesus said, "Come, Peter." Then Peter left the boat and walked on the water to Jesus. But while Peter was walking on the water, he saw the wind and the waves. He was afraid and began sinking into the water. He shouted, "Lord, save me!" Then Jesus caught Peter with his hand. He said, "Your faith is small. Why did you doubt?"

– Matt 14: 28-31 ERV

I went to pick Marc up from after school care and he got in the car as usual. We turned out onto the street. Marc murmured something that I could not make out as he pointed to the light in front of us.

"What did you say, Marc? Are you looking at the light?"

"Light." Marc pointed again to the light as I pulled to it and stopped. "Sssttopp."

"Yes Marc, the light is red, and mommy is stopping."

I watched him as he watched the light. His eyes were fixed on the light, and he waited as if he would miss something big if he moved his eyes away for a split second. Then in a deep voice, I heard "GO!" He said the word giving both the "G" and the "O" an extremely hard sound. Making sure he formed his lips just right to make the word perfect.

Startled, I smiled and said, "Yes, Marc. It is time for mommy to go because the light has turned green. Marc, that is a good job. Mommy is so proud of you!"

As the car ride home continued, every time I was stopped by a red light, Marc told me to stop. He would watch the light like a hawk watching its next prey. When the light turned green, I made sure not to move until Marc said "Go!" Each time, he would look at me with a big smile, waiting for me to reward him with the words, "Good job baby. Mommy is so proud of you!"

LESSON LEARNED:

As I started thinking about the events of the day, I realized that my child did something huge. He learned something, remembered, comprehended, and understood what stop and go meant and the relationship of stop and go to red and green. My child now understood what to do when a light was red. He now understood that lights were there for a reason and were not just street decoration. He was pointing to the light and now knows that when the light is in front of him, he must pay attention to it and do exactly what it tells you to do.

This may not amaze many people, but as a parent of a 10-year-old child with autism who is getting ready to enter middle school, this is huge. He gets it and has the ability to "get" so much more. This is just the beginning of so much more in his life's journey. The doors have been opened. Wow! This is HUGE!

THE LITTLE CAN'S

And my God will meet all your needs according to the riches of
his glory in Christ Jesus.

– Philippians 4:19

We went to Marc's IEP meeting, sat down, and listened to all they had to say. It seemed as though there were 100's of goals for Marc to accomplish in one school year. It was so overwhelming. My son was now 7 years old, and, in the past, he never fulfilled all these goals. I sat there and thought, I just cannot continue to be disappointed. They give him all these big goals and then when he does not reach them, they repeat them on the next IEP and then add to it. Why? Why set myself up for failure? Why set him up for failure? I had to say something.

"Okay," I began, "I understand you all have to fill out every line and every question, but can we please just be honest?"

Everyone just stopped and stared at me.

"These objectives are just too much. All of this stuff for him to do in one year."

Looking stunned, a member of the IEP team said, "We don't think he will do these things 100%, but it will give us something to strive for."

"Okay, so can we strive for something that we know he will achieve? Let me give you some examples: Marc cannot turn the knob to open a door, so let's work on his grip. Marc is not using the bathroom. He is still in a pull up. Let's work on that. Marc knows his numbers and can recognize them so can he add them? Let's work on that. Marc knows his letters and can recognize each sound. Let's work on him learning how to blend the letters and sounds to form words. Can we please be a bit more realistic?"

Another team member said, "I know your concerns and we will add those things for his teacher, but for the IEP we have to look at the big goals."

I said nothing else during that meeting. After the meeting I spoke to Marc's teacher.

"I understand everything about the IEP, but I would like to see some positive advancement so can we work together on one thing this year?" "Sure," she said.

And we looked at one another and said, "Potty Training."

It took almost half the school year, but we were successful. His teacher put him on a schedule at school and I put him on one at home. He went to the bathroom the same time every day. We were consistent and persistent. It became his routine. He started using the bathroom by himself. No more pull-ups! No more wipes! Marc had achieved a goal!

As for all the other goals on his IEP, well the same thing happened. Same goals the next year.

LESSON LEARNED:

It is important to communicate what your child cannot accomplish yet. It is important to be able to celebrate achievements, no matter how minor others may think they are. So what? Marc may not be able to cut with scissors in a straight line. I am 47 and I still must concentrate to do that! So what? Marc may not be able to write in between the lines on a piece of paper and may use three lines. He CAN cut with scissors. He CAN write. He CAN use the bathroom by himself. He CAN and he DOES and that is enough for me!!

WHY "MOMMY" MATTERS

For we are saved by hope: but hope that is seen is not hope: for what a man seeth, why doth he yet hope for? But if we hope for that we see not, then do we with patience wait for it.

– Romans 8: 24-25

There are some words that Marc can speak clearly. There are other words that we just cannot make out. When he wants to use the computer he says, "Compewter?" If we say, "Yes Marc, computer," he says, "Compewter Yas, go?" Then we say, "Yes, go."

When Marc wants juice, he walks up to use and says, "Joose."

If we reply, "Yes Marc, you may have some juice." He goes to the kitchen and opens the refrigerator. If we have to pour it, he puts it on the table and will pick up the first cup he sees. If it is a juice pouch, he will just open the refrigerator, get it out and bring it over to us and whisper, "Open."

I hear Marc at times in his room playing by himself. He says many words that I can make out. He plays with a ball and throws it in the air and says, "Basquetball." He plays with all his different action figures and says things like, "I gotchu," or makes sound effects while clanging them against one another.

Our favorite is when we say, "Buzz, I am your father."

Marc quietly replies, "NOOOOOOooooo." His voice drops like someone running away.

By the end of 2011, Marc had not said mommy. We

would point to all of the family, and he would name them, but when it came to me, he would just smile. He just would not say mommy when asked who I was. I remember telling friends how Marc would not say my name. At first, it upset me. I remember going into my bedroom and crying. Why would he not say my name? Why would he not say mommy? I would even be okay with ma, mom, mama, Patrice at this point. But Marc just would not. He had no problem saying daddy, Sean, Kobe, Grand daddy, Grandma (which he now pronounces "Grandmamama.") and he would even say Tatiana; but would not say a simple mommy. I knew it was not because he couldn't, he just didn't want to, so I thought. You see, Marc would mimic everything someone said to him. So, if someone said the word mommy in conversation, he would repeat it with no hesitation. But if someone asked, "who is she?" while pointing to me, the word mommy would not come out of his mouth, He would just smile at me in his loving way.

Then all of a sudden, in 2012, one of his teachers pointed to me and said, "Marc, who is that?" He looked at me, smiled, and said "Mommeeee." I stopped in my tracks; my son had finally said my name when someone pointed to me. I wanted to jump up and down with joy. Of course, the tears started streaming down my face. To me, it had finally registered with him. I thought, he finally recognized who I am.

But I think truly, Marc knew who I was all along. It was said in his smile when he looked at me after someone asked him who I was. It was said in the times he came to me while I was confused and frustrated and hugged me. It was said in the times he tightly gripped my hand because he was afraid to walk into an unfamiliar place.

I concentrated so much on him saying the words that I missed him showing me who I really was to him. I just wanted to hear the word, "mommy." I had missed that I was so much more to him. He looked at me for something that maybe that one word could not explain. Even though I referred to myself as mommy whenever I spoke to him, hugged him, rocked him, prayed with him, and explained concepts to him; he saw me as more. Or maybe on that day, he just thought, okay I'll give this lady what she wants to hear. So here it goes! But either way, I thank God for the journey.

Some people may think this is just a child who is stubborn. Or maybe, this is a child who just didn't want to say mommy when asked who I was. Some may say why did I make a big deal out of it? Why make the word "mommy" so important or so deep?

To answer that, as a mother of a child with autism, it seems like in a flash he lost so much. One day he was speaking words, sentences, and having conversations. The next nothing. Words that he once said were no longer there. Words that we take for granted were not heard again. We prayed, and prayed, and prayed for the little miracles. Days, months, and years would go by, and we kept praying for the little miracles. Just for the little signs that Marc would regain everything that had been lost. For us, every little thing became a BIG thing. Every little accomplishment became a mountain moved by the hand of God. Why? Because I had to hold on to HOPE. I still hold on to that hope. I cannot let it go. I find hope in what Marc achieves and what he has not achieved yet. It is important for me to not lose hope. So yes, it is a big deal that he did not say my name when people asked him who I was because it kept me praying and relying on my faith through hope. It is because I know where my hope comes from, I look to God for all my answers and continue to hope.

LESSON LEARNED:

Hold on to hope. Never let it go. Do not allow others to steal it from you. They cannot take, what you don't freely give. I was told Marc will never do some things again. I was told that scientifically Marc will never speak words in sentences because that part of his brain has stopped developing. You will be told many things, but God. He is a God that tells us to hope because it is through hope that our faith is strengthened. Find hope in everything, both good and bad. The little things are important. There is a purpose for every little thing that occurs in our life. Look to that purpose and in it your hope, your faith, your love, your patience, your joy, your strength will be made stronger.

Weeping may endure for a night, but joy cometh in the morning. – Psalms 30:5

THE COMFORTER

Come to me, all you who are weary and burdened, and I will give you rest.

– Matthew 11:28

I went in to check on the children before I went to bed, and when I saw Marc, I had a flash back. Before Marc was diagnosed with Autism, his doctor gave me a script for him to see a speech and occupational therapist. Marc had numerous ear infections as a baby and toddler. He had almost lost hearing in one ear. My new pediatrician immediately recommended tubes for his ears. At the same time, Marc began his regression. He had stopped talking and started to just stare. We also noticed he was having trouble holding things like his sippy cup. He had a hard time manipulating his spoon and fork. He also could not turn simple things like a doorknob or even some of the pieces on his toys. So, my pediatrician first wanted to explore the possibility that the regression was part of the hearing loss coupled with some late development, so she wanted to see if he made progress with therapy.

Marc loved occupational therapy. The therapist would use a piece of material that was fitted and snug. She would put Marc in it, and he would stretch and stretch. Then he would curl up in the fetal position like a baby in the womb. After that, she could get him to sit still for other things like practicing turning knobs and handles on different toys. His favorite thing to do was the swing. He would swing and swing and swing. He would often get upset when it was time to get off the swing because that was where he found himself at peace. I look back now and think many times he was probably rocking in the arms of the Lord.

Marc also loved the weighted vest and the weighted blanket. It was as if Marc was truly centered when he had one of those on. He would immediately calm down and look at the therapist directly in the eyes. As a matter of fact, he would get to use those near the end of his session, right before he went into speech therapy, so he would stay focused.

I remember Marc coming home one evening. We were all tired and everyone wanted to go to sleep. Marc would not go to sleep. This was always a problem with Marc, getting to sleep. He just would not fall asleep. He tossed and turned, made noises, screamed a few times, shrieked, and did whatever he could out of frustration. I was at my whit's end on this night. I did not know what to do. I was getting frustrated, annoyed, and upset. I thought I was really going to lose my mind. This was one of the times I asked, "Why me Lord?" I said, "I can't handle this! Why me and why now?" And then, my answer came. I got up and grabbed a heavy blanket my husband had purchased when he was on deployment. I went to Marc's room, took off the comforter that was on his bed and put the blanket on top of him. I tucked it under him, just like the occupational therapist did with the weighted blanket. He looked up at me, smiled, and began to calm down. I gave him pressure (this was a big bear hug) like the therapist had shown me which helps him calm down and focus. I think I must have held him for five minutes. When I let go, he was asleep with the most peaceful look on his face. From that night in 2003 till this day, Marc must have that blanket. He now, at the age of 17, gets his blanket and rolls himself in it to put himself to sleep.

As I look at him tonight, rolled in his blanket with only

his head sticking out; I remember where we came from. I remember the long nights with him up screaming, yelling, and crying. I remember being tempted to scream myself and asking God why me? I remember wanting to just pull my hair out. As I look at Marc now, I see a child that just wanted a closeness. A child that wanted to literally feel love. A child that wanted to feel secure.

LESSON LEARNED:

As I look at myself now, I hear God saying, "Why you? Why not you? Just as Marc is wrapped in that blanket, so are you wrapped in the safety of My arms. Marc is just showing you how I protect and keep you. Just rest in Me and I will give you peace."

PATIENCE, HOPE, FAITH

Our God is in the heavens, and he does as he wishes.

– Psalm 115:3

Someone asked me recently if I had prayed for patience. There is a saying, "never pray for patience. If you do, you are going to have to endure some things to make patience grow in you."

Well, my answer is no, I never prayed for patience. I believe patience is just something God thought I would need in my life when he gave me Marc.

Having a child with any special need requires the gift of patience and is a guaranteed remedy for the lack of patience. Now I am not saying that I am the most patient person in the world. Nor am I saying that my lessons in patience are over. But what I can say is, I believe I have more patience now than previously.

Now, it may not be just because of Marc, but I know God has used him mightily to help my growth. To have a child that is fourteen and has just learned how to tie his shoe, requires patience. To ask a child a question and know he may or may not be able to respond, requires patience. To try and understand how your child's day in school went by catching some words or phrases between the gibberish, requires patience. But bigger than the patience, outweighing it by leaps and bounds, is the feeling of hope.

So, as I think about this, is my lesson one about patience or about hope? Is patience a gift that I am receiving while I learn about having hope. Hope that one day, Marc will hold a conversation about his day. Hope that one day, and one day soon, Marc will be able to bathe himself, pick out his own clothes, brush his own teeth, and brush his hair all on his own. Hope that God is not done with him or me yet.

LESSON LEARNED:

It's funny how we think we know everything and understand how and why things work the way they do. We try and reason with why and how everything happens. I think the real lesson is: Just let God be God. We just need to go along for the ride, knowing and believing God will never leave us or fail us. In all and through all, He is building us to have TRUE faith, obedience, and trust in HIM.

THE RIGHT FIT!

The Lord directs the steps of the godly. He delights in every detail of their lives.

– Psalm 37:23 NLT

We moved to another city in Florida for what we thought was going to be for financial gain, and it ended up being for an investment that was very precious to my family. It was for Marc and his development. This was Marc's time to shine and release the language skills that he had inside him and was initially reluctant to share. Then things changed. We had to move back to the city and county that we had just left which by the way had higher student to teacher ratios and a failing school system. What would we do now? We did not have a lot of time, so it was all about moving and finding the right school that would fit Marc's needs, skills, mindset, and desires. I wanted a school that would allow Marc to develop at his pace in the things he found important, interesting, and relevant. How would I go about this without hindering him? Could I get it done fast enough before regression set in?

Marc started school in our new area which had an autism spectrum unit. We had to move him out of this school quickly. We then found a charter school that specialized in children with autism. He remained there for a year and learned how to use the bathroom by himself while there. However, that was still not the right school for him. Although he did not regress, he did not advance in any other academic or social area and was not happy. We moved once again; this time it was because my husband lost his job. We enrolled Marc into the public school zoned for our new area. This was it! This was the right fit!

Marc began to consistently improve in areas of behavior, speech, comprehension, social skills, and academics. It was not that any of the previous schools were bad, or that they had poor teachers; it was that the teachers, administration, school setting, teaching strategies, and environment had to be the right fit for Marc. Marc was a round peg and he just needed to find the round school that he fit in to. He could not fit in the square or the triangular shaped school. We had to find that round one just for him.

LESSON LEARNED:

Sometimes we see things as failure, but they are really opportunities and lessons. Find the lesson and the journey will be more exciting.

SEEING MYSELF THROUGH THE PAPER

"...Let any one of you who is without sin be the first to throw a stone at her."

– John 8:7 NIV

Everyday Marc comes home, he grabs a piece of paper and a pen, marker, or crayon and just starts drawing on the paper. What does he draw? Well, to me, it looks like a bunch of people walking. But on some of the people he gets really detailed with their facial expressions. Their eyes may be slanted downward with a frown, or they may have a big red smile on their face. I noticed lately that he can just sit and draw and draw and draw without stopping.

I decided to give him a one subject notebook so that he would not use up all the typing paper. He sat down with the notebook and some markers and drew on every page within ten minutes. He then went over to the printer and asked for more paper. Well, I thought, that did not work. If I left any paper within his reach that had blank space on it, he would draw on it. I had to remove the paper out of the printer and put the markers out of his reach. I was thinking he was doing really well because he asked for paper and markers and at least I was in control of how many papers he could draw on and made sure he put the markers away when he was done…and then the day came.

Kobe had to color for his pre-school homework. We gave Kobe the markers. Well, we forgot to put them back up. I came home from school on one of my late nights and when I opened the door, Marc met me with a big hug. I was so pleased. He usually does not even acknowledge that I walked in the door. As I approached the kitchen, I looked on the table and there were papers full of "little people" in all different colors, shapes, and sizes. My husband looked up at me with a smile and said, "Yeah, Marc is hugging you because he did something."

I looked down at Marc and said, "What did you do?"

He looked up at me and said, "Hug?" and walked toward me with his arms opened wide. As he wrapped his arms around me, I followed my husband's eyes to the kitchen table and looked at the papers more carefully. It was my work. There were all my papers with "little people" all over them. As Marc was hugging me, he must have felt the change in my body language. He immediately released and said, "Mommy h-u-g."

I hugged him and then both of our smiles returned. "Marc, that's okay. Mommy can print out a new one. I am not mad at you."

He looked up at me with a bigger smile than before. I smiled back. Upon seeing that smile from me, he let go and ran to his sister's room to watch television. Knowing I was not upset with him, allowed him to continue on with his day.

My husband looked up at me and said, "Wow, now I know the trick."

My daughter finished his thought, "Yeah daddy, just ask mommy for a hug when you think you're getting in trouble."

I realized then; Marc taught me something in that moment. He helped me grow up a little in that moment.

LESSON LEARNED:

It is hard sometimes to see past what someone has done

to me and look at what I did to contribute to their actions. I had left the papers out in Marc's reach. What I had to realize is that I could not get mad at Marc without being mad with myself. It is harder to recognize my contribution to a bad situation before I let anger set in and move in my emotions. If I would have put up my papers and the markers like I tell my children to put up their toys, then Marc would not have written all over them. I think back and wonder, how many things would line up if I would just do what I am supposed to do. If I could concentrate more on getting myself in order, then everything and everyone else would have to fall in line.

Believe me, I am not saying I got this down, but I am saying I have learned that I do need to be willing to see myself and correct me.

JUST MAGNIFIED

"I knew you before I formed you in your mother's womb. Before you were born I set you apart and appointed you as my prophet to the nations."

– Jeremiah 1:5 NLT

A lot of times when I watch Marc, I see myself. A lot of times when I watch myself, I see Marc. Why when I do it, the doctors do not see autism but when he does it, he is autistic?

I get so excited sometimes that I lose all words and flail my hands. I may also jump up and down a few times to show the level of my excitement. I roll myself up in blankets at night to fall asleep no matter how hot it may be in the house. When I cannot think of what to write or say, I may hold my head with both hands and contemplate. If I want my husband's attention, I may jump up and down like a little girl. I am full of energy and life. I smile all the time. I sometimes find myself standing in the kitchen over a cookie sheet of day-old fries eating them one by one. When I am misunderstood or disappointed or mad, I may have a temper tantrum. I love to watch commercials and remember slogans to ad campaigns. I love numbers and mathematics and love to figure out puzzles no matter how difficult. I have a hard time being still or just doing one thing until it is finished. I must do multiple things at once. When I am eating, I tend to rock back and forth.

Now let's compare:

When Marc gets excited, he flails his hands and makes

a noise to show his excitement. He may also jump up and down to get your attention to make others aware of his level of excitement. When he does it, it can annoy people around. They believe he is acting out of character for a "normal" nine-year-old boy. When I do it, I am considered dramatic or overly emotional. Marc rolls himself up in his blankets when he goes to sleep. When he does it, it is considered a calming mechanism. Therapists have told us it is helping him cope with the transition from activity to no activity. Marc used to take his hand and hit himself once on the head with an open palm when he could not figure out something. When he did this, he was considered to be harming himself. When I hold my head or see others do the same as Marc, it is considered a tactic they use to show and cope with frustration. Marc memorizes movies, mostly Disney. When he does it, we are told he is mimicking and just repeating instead of vocabulary development. When I do it, people just think I have favorite commercials that I have just remembered. I could go on and on with this list of comparisons, but I will not. I just look back and realize his actions are just mine magnified.

Why is he diagnosed with Autism and I am not? I believe it is because I can turn mine on and off and his is always on. How do we fix it? How do we install that switch for him? What made his switch stop working? Why is it different for me than it is for him?

These questions may never be answered, but I can say I love knowing he is his mother's child…and his dad's too (I just did not want to embarrass his dad with those similarities).

See I heard it said many times, "Your children are ten times what you were as a child."

Well, I got one that was magnified a little bit more than ten times and guess what:

I LOVE EVERY MOMENT OF OUR LIFE'S JOURNEY.

LESSON LEARNED:

It became surprising and comforting when I notice myself in my child especially when that child is diagnosed with Autism. It became a sign that it really is not as big of a "problem" as some would want me to believe. My child is just his dad and myself magnified.

Love yourself and love the parts of you that your child has chosen to magnify because you have a child that loves you for ALL of you.

GOING BACKWARD

"God is our refuge and strength, A very present help in trouble."

– Psalms 46:1

Sometimes I think Marc is just going backward. He has made a lot of progress when it comes to his language skills, but then suddenly, his social skills go the other way. He started having tantrums for no reason again. In the car, he started rocking very fast. Back and forth. Then he tried to apply pressure using his younger brother (3 years old at the time) by pressing his mouth onto Kobe's arm as hard as possible.

It comes out of nowhere.

When I tell him, he cannot have a snack, he starts to hit himself on the leg, or even scratch himself. He then looks at me and cries while saying. "Sahwy Marc."

All these behaviors I thought had left, but they come back.

Is it because he is ten and approaching puberty? Do children with Autism enter puberty earlier? How does puberty affect children with Autism who are already extremely sensitive to touch? Will he be able to control the emotions that come with an increased testosterone level as well as those that come with Autism. I guess I shall see.

In the meantime, I am just going to continue to be consistent. I will give him hugs and love him no matter what. I cannot imagine the emotional changes Marc is going through and the changes that are soon to come.

LESSON LEARNED:

One day at a time.

HIS THOUGHTS

"Do not conform to the pattern of this world but be transformed by the renewing of your mind. Then you will be able to test and approve what God's will is—his good, pleasing, and perfect will."
— Romans 12:2 NIV

Sometimes I wonder what goes on in Marc's mind. He cannot communicate it to me with words. So many times, he tries his best to express it with pointing, sounds, gestures, or pictures. This time I was in awe when I discovered a picture he drew.

I purchased a LeapPad for Marc as a Christmas gift. He uses it as a camera and draws on it. I then went out and bought him an android tablet and gave the LeapPad to my daughter who loves to play on it. My daughter needed more shampoo and food for her little virtual pet (a game she played on the device), so I had to plug the LeapPad into the computer. My daughter and I started pulling up the pictures and videos that she, Marc, and my older son Sean had taken. And then it happened! We get to a picture, and it really shocked us. My daughter's eyes were wide, and she opened her mouth wide in amazement. "Wow, mommy who did that?"

I looked and asked, "You didn't do that?"

"No mommy, I don't know how to do that?"

I called Sean over. "Sean, did you do this?"

"Do what mom?" As he walked over, he looked at the picture. "Woah! That is awesome! I think Marc did that!"

"Sean, you did not draw anything on this picture?"

"No mom. Really Marc did that, and he is good! Wow, I did not know Marc could do that! I think he was thinking about Jesus. But why so many crosses?"

I called Marc over and asked, "Did you do this?"

Of course, he looked at me with his cutest smile and said, "you do this?" mimicking my voice and its inflection.

I knew that he was not going to tell me.

However, that smile he had on his face told me the answer was yes, Marc had created it.

I just want to know what he was thinking, what he was hearing while he made his art. he started with a picture of his bed and distorted it (stretched it, warped it, bent it, etc.) to form a piece of art that says so much!!

When you think they are not listening, they are!!

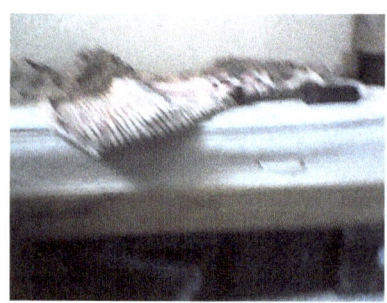
Before

After

LESSON LEARNED:

Sometimes I tend to look for Marc to communicate like me. I want him to say words, phrases, and sentences. I want him to be able to hold a conversation and ask questions about things I am trying to teach him. I learned that I must listen to what Marc is saying through his means of communication. Just because someone does not do things the way the world says they ought, does not mean they are less than or not capable.

THE EVIDENCE IS ON RECORD

"For this reason, since the day we heard about you, we have not stopped praying for you. We continually ask God to !ll you with the knowledge of his will through all the wisdom and understanding that the Spirit gives, so that you may live a life worthy of the Lord and please him in every way: bearing fruit in every good work, growing in the knowledge of God,"
– Colossians 1: 9-10 NIV

One of Marc's favorite things to do is get a book and go page by page looking at the pictures (so we thought). He loved to get the Sunday's paper when he was younger and open different sections and just turn the pages as if he were searching for a new picture to capture his attention. His face would light up when he got to the comics section. He flipped through them and would smile as if he was so tickled by the writers' humor. One day while in the grocery store, we were walking down the aisle with paper products. As we walked by, we could hear a faint sound naming each product we passed. My husband stopped and said, "Is Marc reading the labels?"

I said, "No he can't be. You know he has a good memory. He is just remembering the packaging from the commercials."

My husband looked and went to a package and said, "Marc, what does this say?"

Marc looked up at his daddy then to the package and gave the biggest grin and said...nothing. "See, honey I told you he can't read he's just mimicking the commercials."

The schools that Marc went to never concentrated on reading. They concentrated on him knowing his alphabets and their corresponding sounds, but to put them together to form and recognize individual words was too advance and not addressed at any time on his IEP. His IEP was designed to address things like, holding his pencil properly, putting pressure on paper to write, zipping up a zipper, dressing himself, recognizing some of the alphabets and numbers, working in social settings, staying on tasks, but never anything as challenging as reading, or mathematics. So, why would I expect him to read if I knew that was not the focus at school? Well, I guess just because it was not my focus or the school's focus does not mean it was not Marc's focus.

This year, 2011, Marc took his assessment test (which I think is so silly for students that are non-verbal and in special units to have to take state mandated testing) and surprised us all. His teacher called me and said, "You will not believe what happened during the test today!"

I am waiting for the bad report, so I hesitantly said, "What happened?"

She was overjoyed; her voice was trembling from excitement and disbelief. "Marc read the stories in the test to me. I did not help him at all. I was ready to read them to him like I am supposed to and when he saw the words; he started to read them to me!! And then when he got to the questions, I asked him the questions and he answered them with no help from me and guess what?" Before I could speak, she said, "They were the right answers!!! Did you know Marc can read?"

"No, I did not know. I mean there were signs, but no one taught him so, no, I did not know."

"Well, he can, and I am going to push him in that

direction to see how much he knows."

Score reports came in and Marc was the highest scorer in his class. His scores improved over 110% from the previous year in Reading and Mathematics. So now when Marc looks through a book one page at a time looking like he is really captivated by the story that is unfolding before his eyes; I know that he is really reading those words. Although, he still will not read out loud to myself or his dad and he still just gives us that same smile when we ask him to read something; the evidence is now on record.

My baby that still has his challenges with forming complete sentences can read. Just one more of life's journeys that he has tackled.

LESSON LEARNED:

They may act like they are not getting it, but they are. Do not get frustrated just keep loving them and keep repeating if you must. Believe it or not, it is in there. Allow your child to decide when and if they want to release it but know in your mind that it is in there like a little seed and growing.

JUST SOMETHING HE DOES

"For we are his workmanship, created in Christ Jesus for good works, which God prepared beforehand, that we should walk in them."

– Ephesians 2:10 ESV

When I clean up Marc's room, I have stopped being surprised with what I find. Well, most of the time anyway. I know Marc loves to "stim" with paper.

If you have a child with autism, "stimming" is a term that you are probably very familiar with. It is the act of someone stimulating one or more senses by repetition of some type of movement. For some children it is the constant rocking back and forth motion. For some children it is a slight movement with their fingers, feet, or other extremity. For Marc it just does not involve movement, but it involves movement with an object...paper. Marc tares any piece of paper until it is just the right size. He then rolls it using his fingers. He folds and bends it to form shapes or animals (horses are his favorite), he begins slowly at first. He makes it fly, hop, and just any type of motion. After a while he pulls the paper closer to one eye, the closer the better. When he gets the paper at that perfect distance from his eye (he closes one eye and moves the paper back and forth to make sure it is in the perfect position) then the stimming begins. He makes clicking sounds, snorts, grind his teeth, and at some points he sounds off in a high screech.

When does it happen? Whenever Marc feels he needs stimulation of his senses.

Why does it happen? I do not know.

How do I correct it? I do not know.

At times I know that he uses it as a calming mechanism. When we go to a new doctor, or when he walked into a new school on the first day, I allow him to have the paper to calm him. In these instances, he usually does not get loud, he just continues to roll the paper in between his fingers. Please do not get me wrong, there are the times that Marc does it because he sees paper. At those times, stimming is discouraged. I ask, "What do you have?" He brings me the paper, sometimes reluctantly when he knows it's something, he should not have torn. I then say put it in the trash and he does. Did it start out this way? OH NO!!!!

I remember when I would say, "No Marc don't do that. Now go put the paper in the trash." Marc would resist with the loudest, highest pitched squeal. He would then do things like fall to the floor, or hit himself on the leg, or run through the house screaming. Oh my, do I remember. We have come so far. It is now a routing for Marc. He knows if mom did not give him the paper, then he should not have the paper, so what did he do? He found a hiding spot...behind and under his bed.

As I said in the beginning, cleaning up Marc's side of his bedroom has stopped yielding as many surprises as possible. Things I have found torn to shreds and formed into shapes and animals are money, checks, pages from books, letters, candy wrappers, wrappings off plastic straws, pieces of erasers, post it notes (his favorite), pieces of ear plugs, wire from one or more of my earrings that he has taken apart, paperclips, paper plates, aluminum foil, and much more. If it's missing and it's made of anything that can come apart and form a shape or object, we check under Marc's bed first. It used to frustrate me, but I have learned that it's just something he does. Just like some people suck their thumb, suck on their teeth, bite their nails, grind their teeth, constantly lick their lips, say the words "like" and "Um" 50,000 times while they talk; Marc is no different.

LESSON LEARNED:

At times it can become very frustrating trying to correct a child with autism, especially with some of the behaviors that are not seen as "normal." At times you may just want to give in because of their reactions to your correction but hold your ground. Know what they will do and stop them before they do it. I knew that Marc was going to either fall to the ground, hit himself, run, and/or scream so I was prepared. After I told him to put it in the trash, I would do things like sit him on the couch and sit down beside him and read or give him a car to play with to replace that paper, or just tell him he did a good job and reinforce the behavior with something that he liked. Repetition must occur until learning takes place. Many things did not come to us after our first experience. It took some type of repetition for all of us to learn some of life's lessons. Keep going and do not give up, it will happen.

LOOKING BACK AND STARTING NEW

"I will bless the Lord at all times: his praise shall be continually in my mouth."

– Psalms 34:1 KJV

The end of the school year is here and so is the end of Marc's learning with whom I believe to be the best teacher. This is a sad time for me. He has come so far with his teacher. He has advanced and excelled with his speech and communication. He has hit some of his targets on his IEP. He shows he understands me by responding appropriately. He has worked very hard, and I am so proud of him.

Today I said, "Marc, can you get me some chips?"

He opened the pantry and reached in the bag and got me out a bag of Doritos.

I said, "No Marc, I don't want those. Try another one."

He put those back and got me a bag of Frito's.

"No Marc, not those."

He reached in the bag and got me a bag of Sun Chips.

"No Marc, try again."

He began to laugh. Now this was getting funny to him. He put the bag back in the pantry and closed the door.

"Wait Marc, I need my chips. Look in the bag for more."

He opened the pantry and looked in the bag. I stood up beside him to assist him by holding the bag at an angle so that he could see the selection that was inside. He smiled and touched the Cheetos.

"Yes Marc! Mommy loves Cheetos!"

He smiled and gave me the bag, closed the pantry, and stood beside me.

"Thank you so much Marc. You made mommy happy."

He smiled and walked away happy to his room.

Three years ago, two years ago, even six months ago, Marc would not have done that. I would have probably gotten so frustrated because he was not understanding me and resorted to getting the chips myself. But now, it is so different. The frustration was not there. He understood me the first time I said each thing. I did not have to repeat myself! Wow, what an accomplishment.

So, what, he can't tie his shoe? So, what, I have to help him brush his teeth? So, what, he only reads on a first-grade level? He is improving, he is learning, he is growing in God's time to be someone great!

As I am looking back, I can only take joy in thinking about what is to come in his Life's Journey.

LESSON LEARNED:

Although his learning may have taken awhile, according to me, I must rejoice that he is learning. I have learned that saying "So What?" is okay because the "Marc Can's" are bigger and greater. "So What's" become "Marc Can's!"

THE WRENCH IN THE ROUTINE

"Trust in the LORD with all your heart and lean not on your own understanding; in all your ways submit to him, and he will make your paths straight."

– Psalm 3:5-6 NIV

Like many people diagnosed with autism, Marc likes consistency and routine. I noticed that he now handles breaks from school much better than he did before. Currently, he can have a break during Thanksgiving, Christmas, even the summer and return to school with no problem, whereas breaks used to present a huge problem for Marc, the teacher, and his classmates. What Marc still requires assistance with are the unexpected changes in his routines. The changes that pop out of nowhere and just do not make sense to him. On one Sunday the unexpected change occurred.

We go to church in the morning and when we arrive home, Marc takes off his church clothes, puts on some lounge clothes and begins to play in his room or on the computer. This is his Sunday routine. This is what is supposed to happen every Sunday. One Sunday we got home from church and Marc began to take off his clothes, I told him he had to keep his clothes on. Marc looked confused, "No!"

I looked at him and said, "Marc, do not take off your clothes. We are going somewhere later so keep your clothes on."

Marc became upset. He began to make a loud moaning cry and ran to his room tugging on his clothes. I followed him in his room and said, "Marc, we are going out. You must keep on your clothes. You need to calm down."

Marc repeated me with tears coming down his eyes, "Calm down."

"Yes, Marc calm down. It is okay."

Marc looked at me and said, "Hug!"

I hugged him and said, "Happy" with a smile on my face.

Marc imitated my smile and said, "Happy."

Marc saw that everything was going to be okay. We went out and he had a great time. When he got home, he looked at me and tugged on his shirt and said, "Off?"

I told him he could take his clothes off. After he put on his lounge gear, he ran to the computer, and everything was back to normal for him.

LESSON LEARNED:

Sometimes things do not go as planned. Sometimes there may be a little "wrench" thrown into our normal routine. It may not be something huge, just something big enough (or small enough) to change our usual course for a moment.

I remember, I had made plans with funds I was due to get. The money did not come on that day. I lost it. God saw me as having that moaning cry and temper tantrum.

God looked down on me and said, "Patrice, calm down."

My experience with Marc taught me something. God may not sit down with us and explain the why, but just as I wanted Marc to trust that everything would be okay because I am his mother and I love him and would do nothing to hurt him, God wants us to understand that he feels the same about us. So, if there was a wrench thrown into the routine, use it to build a new plan. Use it to reveal God's plan.

WHAT TO DO?
"Sing aloud unto God our strength: Make a joyful noise unto the God of Jacob."

– Psalm 81:1

I love Marc's teacher. She is the best! She has a child herself with autism spectrum disorder, so she has more than book knowledge, she has life experience. She has been my rock when Marc is at school. I know that he is well taken care of, and I know that everything we do at home is the same as what is done at school. So, knowing that this is his last year with her is sad and scary.

I now must find a middle school that is right for Marc. This is going to take a lot of time. There are many schools that offer an autism unit, but it is important to find one that will continue to help Marc progress and not digress. I have visited some classrooms where the teachers sit at the desk and in one corner the TV is on, in another corner children are at computers, and then there are some students at their desks playing with toys. This is not the environment that Marc is used to, so to put him there would be a digression. I have visited schools that teach the students about washing clothes, tying shoes, using the bathroom by themselves, and other "life skills." Again, this is not the environment that Marc is used to so to put him there would not help him. This is when parenting becomes most important.

First, I must keep in mind that Marc will be going through a major change from a three-year routine. He will have a different classroom, a different teacher, and different classmates than what he is used to. To change the type of learning that he has grown accustomed to may be too much for him; therefore, if Marc's behavior changes, then it will be understandable.

My mission, then, is to find a school that will challenge him academically as well as allow him the sensory stimulation he needs and that will have both speech and occupational therapy. As I go on my quest, I have to keep in mind Marc's demeanor and temperament. I must find the right fit.

So, a' searching I will go!

LESSON LEARNED:

Keep in mind that sometimes convenience is not always best. We may have to be a little uncomfortable now in order to be comfortable later. When Marc graduates from high school and goes on to college, all my inconveniences will not matter.

A VICTORY FOR MARC,
BY MARC!

"You need not fight in this battle; take your positions, stand and witness the salvation of the Lord who is with you, O Judah and Jerusalem. Do not fear or be dismayed; tomorrow go out against them, for the Lord is with you."
— 2 Chronicles 20:17 AMP

Marc has always loved to draw. He draws things that he sees on his favorite movies and cartoons. He draws all the time. When he draws, he gives it all his energy and time. He concentrates on trying to include every detail. He loosely holds the pencil, crayon, or marker. Then it is off to the races. He moves so quickly, making circles, dots, lines, and shapes. Then he's done, just as quickly as he started. So, why do I write about this? Many children love to draw. What makes Marc any different or special in my eyes? Well, since Marc has autism, he groups things many times by one or two similar characteristics. For example, the paper Marc draws on is white. In school, Marc uses a whiteboard to write and draw on, which by its name, is white. His teachers utilize a Smart Board which is white. So, in Marc's mind, if it's white, he can write on it.

On this day, Marc discovered his walls in his room were white. So, to the walls he went. A wall was bigger and more convenient. It was very similar to a white board. Why not?

My plan was to clean the walls every weekend. I bought bottles of Goof Off, which claimed to remove crayon, marker, tar, and adhesive from walls. And, yes it worked and also provided me with the best upper arm workout I have had in years. Since I didn't sign up for the workout, cleaning the walls stopped shortly after it started.

I punished Marc. I put him in time out. I told him over and over to stop writing on the walls. I even began to hide writing utensils from everyone. But somehow, Marc would manage to find one or bring one home from school and stash it somewhere. I would walk in his room and see a new drawing on the wall weekly. "Marc! You know better! Where is the crayon?" Then of course, I would get the blank stare like he had no idea what I was saying, knowing he knew exactly what he was doing and what I was saying.

Well, I don't know if Marc wore me down, or I realized that it really was not that big of a deal. A wall can be painted. I stopped hiding the writing instruments. I decided that there were bigger battles to fight and conquer, so I decided to just let him do it. He drew only on his side of the room, over his side of the bed. He did not write on his brother's side nor anywhere else in the house.

Then it happened. I noticed there were no new drawings on Marc's wall. I saw him in his room with markers and peeped in. He took the markers and placed them on his bed. He went to the desk in his room where I kept school supplies. He opened the drawer, looked in, and pulled out a new notebook. He closed the drawer with the notebook in hand and went over to his bed, opened the marker, opened the notebook, and back and forth the marker glided on the paper. He quickly turned the page and repeated his actions. He completed all 70 sheets of the notebook without looking up once. After he was done, he put the notebook back in the drawer, closed the marker, looked up at me, and smiled. I hugged him and said, "battle won."

LESSON LEARNED:

Some things they will learn on their own. Choose your battles. Sometimes I exhausted myself fighting battles that really were not that important in the grand scheme of things. I had to begin to ask myself, "What if I lose this battle? Will it put him, myself, or anyone else in harm's way? Is it something that I can live with? Is it something that he can live with? What if it's just not my battle to fight and because I am choosing to fight it for him, he does not get the value out of it?" There are some victories that belong to Marc, not me, and I must allow him the opportunity to have his victories also. I have come to realize: the best victories are the victories he wins with help from the Lord.

BEING IN PLACE

"But the Lord God called to Adam, and said to him, 'Where are you?'"

— Genesis 3:9 AMP

"Then the Lord said to Cain, 'Where is Abel your brother?' And he [lied and] said, 'I do not know. Am I my brother's keeper?'"

— Genesis 4:9 AMP

I have noticed that sometimes when I am back in my room looking at television and Marc is playing by himself or with his siblings, he will pop his head in my room, look around and then go back to doing what he was doing earlier. I noticed that if he goes to a room and I change my location, he will look for me until he finds me, take a quick glance, and goes off on his own again. I never really thought of it much, but when I sat back one day and observed him, it hit me what was really going on.

My father came down to visit us for the week. He stayed with us, so everyone was under the same small roof. We had just come back from eating out, and Marc headed straight to the front bathroom. My husband sat in the living room, I went to the kitchen, and all the other kids went to Sean Jr.'s room and began playing. My father went to the back bathroom. When Marc came out, he immediately walked into the room with his siblings and saw everyone playing. He then smiled and turned around, walked out, and went into the living room. He looked to the left and saw his dad and then looked to the right and saw me in the kitchen. He continued to walk, now on a mission, and looked in Tatiana's room. He looked around the room and stopped. He then walked into the kitchen. He went back into the front bathroom. He then sprinted to the second bathroom and was met by a closed door. He got on his knees and attempted to look under the door. He got back up and turned the doorknob. It was locked. Of course, my father said, "Someone is in here!"

But that did not satisfy Marc. Somehow, someway, Marc unlocked the door. He peeped in and then shut the door quickly. Satisfied, he turned and went into the room to play with his siblings.

My husband looked up at me and said, "Marc wanted to know where his grandaddy was, and was determined to find him."

I began to think about how Marc always walks around the apartment just peeping in rooms to see who is where. I also began to think of how Marc will not go to sleep until the lights are off in the house and everyone is in their proper place for the night. He will stay in his room, in his bed and roll paper to create different people, creatures, or objects while humming until the last light is out. It is as if he must make sure everyone is in their proper place before he puts his head down for the evening. He does the same during the day. Everyone must be in their proper place before he continues about his day.

LESSON LEARNED:

I asked myself, "Am I always where I am supposed to be?" If God came looking for me, would He have to call out, "Patrice, where are you?" or would I be right there in my appointed place, at the appointed time, doing the right thing, with the right people, and in the right mindset and right heart to meet Him?

I continue to thank God for allowing me to be blessed with Marc, a son God uses to allow me to understand His word and His desires more clearly. What an awesome gift God has given each of us who have a person like Marc in our lives. Once we look past ourselves and how autism will or has affected our lives, we can begin to enjoy, appreciate, and understand the person behind the condition as God does. Although this is not easy, and some days are more trying than others, when we get it, even if it is for a minute or two, we really get it. And instead of dreading the next minute, hour, or day, we can begin to look forward to the next lesson we will learn while on this journey in their life.

HIS DAY ON A HORSE

"Come to me, all who labor and are heavy laden, and I will give you rest."

– Matthew 11:28 ESV

Today we took the family horseback riding. Marc has always loved horses and has never been shy around one. Today, when we got to the stables, he was ready to go. First, he walked around the desk trying to go into the stables so he could pick out his own horse. It was as if he knew exactly what to do. I told him they would bring the horse to him. A little confused, he got aggravated. When he turned around and saw the horses waiting for us, his aggravation changed into happiness and joy instantly. I walked him over to his horse. The guide attached him to his horse and off we went. He had no problems. He smiled the entire time. He held the reins loosely, but the horse never veered off track. The horse was so mild tempered and handled nicely unlike my stubborn horse that matched my temperament. We turned around about 30 minutes into the ride to head back and a man on a beautiful black horse came riding by. He turned around and came back to ride beside Marc. Not knowing that Marc had autism and he did not hold conversations with people, he asked, "Are you having fun?"

Marc repeated him, "Having fun?"

The man said, "Do you like the horses?"

Marc replied, "Horses!" with a high pitch of excitement. Marc then pointed at the man's horse and said in a demanding tone, "Run. Horse run."

The man began to laugh and said, "You want me to make my horse run?"

Marc responded, "Run horse. Run horse!" The second one much louder than the first.

The man laughed and said, "Okay, I will do it just for you."

We all pulled to the side and stopped our horses. Marc's guide led him to a place where he could see everything. The male rider turned his horse around and made sure he had Marc's attention.

"Make sure you are watching!" he shouted.

Then with a kick and a lick, the horse took off. The horse kicked up dirt and ran like a horse on a racetrack. Marc's eyes sparkled with joy. His smile was so big.

The man came back, and Marc looked at the man and said, "Horse running and running and running." His imitation of Forest Gump.

It brought a smile to my face (as it does now, remembering this). My baby had a conversation with a stranger freely. I did not have to force him, explain anything to him, re-word anything the man or Marc was saying, or tell him what to say. I wasn't even beside him to guide him even if I needed to. He gave eye contact. He said what he wanted and was understood. WOW!

Later, that evening, Marc came up to me and said, "Cowboy Yaw!"

I said, "Yes baby, cowboy said Yaw!" "Cowboy horse run!"

"Yes, the cowboy made his horse run."

"Horse?"

"Yes, we saw the horses!"

"Horse? Let's go!" and he pointed to the door ready to hear me say yes let's go.

I looked up at him and his bright smile and said,

"Another time baby. We will go see the horses another time."

He was content with that response and went to his room to draw pictures of the cowboy on the horse.

What a wonderful day!

LESSON LEARNED:

There will be days of joy and rest. REMEMBER those days often.

ENTER IN CAUTIOUSLY

"Be well balanced and always alert, because your enemy, the devil, roams around incessantly, like a roaring lion looking for its prey to devour."

— 1 Peter 5:8 TPT

We went to a different library than usual. While we were picking out books, Kobe had to use the restroom. I put the books on the table and told Marc he had to come with me because Kobe needed to go to the restroom, which was not directly inside the library but out in the hallway of the entrance of the library. Marc immediately turned around and walked towards me. The three of us walked out of the double doors and walked a few steps towards the restroom door. When I opened the door, it was dark. Marc stopped. The bathroom was equipped with an automatic light that was triggered by motion. I knew I had to walk into the bathroom so the light would come on. I looked down at Kobe and he had stopped in his tracks too. I stepped around both of them and waved until the light came on. Kobe entered with no problem after seeing it was a legitimate bathroom. Marc on the other hand, was very cautious.

"Come on in Marc, Kobe has to go!"

Marc peeped through the door. Kobe was now holding his stomach.

"Come in now! It's OK." I exclaimed.

Marc slowly walked through the door.

"Mommy, my tummy hurts bad!" Kobe was almost in tears.

As I rushed Kobe into the stall, I turned to make sure Marc had successfully made it inside the restroom. He was so cautious. He checked the large stall first. The next stall was locked from the inside, so he could not check it by simply pushing open the door. Marc went inside the large stall and got on his knees to look under it.

"Marc, get up off of that dirty floor!"

Marc did not budge until he made sure no one was there. When he got up, I asked if he had to use the bathroom. Marc gave me a look that was all too familiar. If Marc needed to use the bathroom he would have just said: "BAFFROOM!" If Marc did not have to use the bathroom he would have said, "NO!"

But he gave me the look! The look meant, even if I did, I am not going to do it here!

The entire time Marc stood by the door, ready to exit. I knew I had to be quick because I have learned not to take Marc's cautiousness for granted.

In 2009, Marc had to be seen by a psychologist so that he could be declared disabled by the government for Social Security benefits. I remember when we arrived at the address of the psychologist's office. The building was a small, white, wooden two-bedroom house that had been converted into an office. Outside of the office was a wooden ramp for wheelchair exit access. Parking was on the side of the house in a lot that was once grass but now was covered with gravel. I parked the car and Marc just looked at the office and the surroundings. I opened the door for Marc, and he got out of the car very slowly, cautiously. As I walked towards the ramp, Marc was looking very carefully and walking extremely slowly. I recall the walk up the ramp. That walk was the longest walk to me. Marc would not budge. He just stopped at the bottom of the ramp. He would not move. I took him by his arm and began to pull him up the ramp. He continued to resist. At some point I wrapped my arm around his waist and pushed him up the ramp. The entire time, his eyes were wide, and his face looked as if he knew something that I did not. He was truly frightened. I finally got him up to the door, and as I opened it, Marc ducked his head behind me.

At that moment I stopped and said a quick prayer. "Father, protect us from all dangers unseen. Amen."

I opened the door, and Marc ducked all the way behind me and closed his eyes. There was a small waiting area with burgundy chairs. We went in. There was a closed door with a sign on it that led to the remainder of the house. The sign read: "In a session, please be quiet and have a seat."

I recall thinking, "Be quiet? I have a child with autism, how am I going to keep him quiet?"

I sat down in one of the chairs and Marc immediately sat on my lap, kicked his feet to the side of my legs, and hugged me like he was a baby again. Marc waited patiently and the entire time did not mumble a word.

When it was our time to be seen, a man came out and called us back. Again, I had to pull Marc through the door. We entered an office with large dark furniture. The rest of the house was now open to us and we could see a large dark dining table and much more dark furniture. I sat down in a chair opposite the psychologist's desk, and although there was an empty chair beside me, Marc squeezed into my chair. The psychologist began to talk to Marc. Marc did not say a word. Not one! I answered all the questions and described Marc's usual behavior, but Marc would not take his eyes off me. After I finished, the psychologist began to write his report. Marc then quickly looked up; I followed his eyes. He looked behind the psychologist in a huge cabinet which contained many different knickknacks and continued to stare for a while. He then turned back to me. I just didn't get it!

Marc had never acted like this before. When the psychologist thanked me for coming in, he turned to a side door that we were to leave out of, but Marc was not having it. He began to shrill. I told the psychologist that we had to leave the way we came. He allowed us.

As I left, I began to take notice of all the little things that were lying around, and I got a closer look at the large cabinet that was behind his desk. It was then clear to me. The statues, the knickknacks, and the pictures that were all around were a clear display that this office was full of things that were not in agreement with the God I serve. Marc ran out the door in front of me. He ran down the ramp and to the car. He got in the car and as we drove away, he started acting himself again.

LESSON LEARNED:

So many times, we go into the unknown fully exposed. We forget to pray before we enter in. Sometimes we go into the dark willingly, ignoring the actions of God that are trying to stop us and warn   us that there are knickknacks not like Him there. We don't look around cautiously and inspect the place.

We let people into our lives without inspection.
The words from their mouth may sound good, but all the signs that they have displayed and all the knickknacks around them are contrary to what they say and what we believe, but we let them in anyway.

The places that we go may seem innocent, but all the signs that are displayed in all the knickknacks lying around are contrary to what we believe, but we enter in any way. God continues to tug on us to stop us, but we try to push Him in with us. We try to force Him to enter in. We must realize that He stops at the door. He does not enter in with us.

Light and dark cannot be in the same place at the same time. Through Marc, God has taught me to take notice.

From that day, I realized not to take Marc's reluctance as just a bad behavior, but to value it and give it the attention that it deserves.

I have a son with autism. I have a son that sees, feels and thinks things that are beyond my understanding. I have a son who does not know how to communicate those things to me verbally, so he does the best that he can with his actions. I must pay attention.

We cannot immediately jump to conclusions when our children act out. We cannot immediately assume, "Here they go again!" We cannot just brush it off and tell everyone, "He/She is acting like that because they have autism."

We have to stop and listen to what they're trying to say to us before we react. It is an easy thing to say but a hard thing to do. Believe me, I am still working on this one.

THE BLAME GAME

"My fellow believers, when it seems as though you are facing nothing but difficulties, see it as an invaluable opportunity to experience the greatest joy that you can!
For you know that when your faith is tested it stirs up in you the power of endurance. And then as your endurance grows even stronger, it will release perfection into every part of your being until there is nothing missing and nothing lacking."
— James 1: 2-5 TPT

This morning as Marc was trying to talk to me, I began to thank God for all his advancements, and I recalled how we felt when we first found out he had autism. We played the blame game. We started looking back over things we had done and wondered could there be a reason he had autism. I think as parents and loved ones, we all do this.
My thoughts were:

1. I should have gotten the amniocentesis when I had a chance. Maybe that would have told me something. But if it could, which it does not, what would I have been able to do about it? What would I have done? NOTHING.

2. Maybe if I were more attentive to him when he was a baby, he would not have autism. Maybe if I didn't sit him in the bouncer in front of the television as much, he would be better. He really liked the bright colors and singing, but maybe that was just too much stimulation for him. But can I change that

now? NO!

My husband once told me he thought:

1. If he did not miss those first six months of Marc's life when we were separated, then maybe he would have noticed it. Maybe he would have caught it and we could have done something earlier. But what could we have done? NOTHING! Even our pediatrician did not want to diagnose Marc too early. She waited to make sure.

2. Could this possibly be his fault for the past sins he committed? Maybe, Marc's autism was my husband's punishment? But having a child with autism is not a punishment.

Everyone's thoughts:

Is there something in either of our families that we didn't know about? Is this hereditary and we didn't know it?

I think at one time or another we all have done this blame game. I know I've tried to blame it on parents, genetics, television, nutrition, immunizations, etc. But why must I blame?

I had to get over the blame game and realize that having a child with autism is a gift from God. It is a preparation for me as a parent to acquire all the skills that I need to fulfill my purpose. It is a chance for me as a parent to understand how children perceive things and how their minds develop. It is an opportunity for Marc to connect to things on a much higher level that I cannot imagine. He sees things, he notices things, and he is aware of things that I can't fathom. He is honest because he doesn't understand the concept of lying. He follows my directions to the T. He is so organized. He is extremely trusting; he doesn't even understand the concept of danger sometimes. He loves without judgment. If I could only say the same things about myself!

Sometimes I watch Marc as he tries to communicate with me. On some days I just don't get it. On those days he screams, yells, and becomes angry with me. Sometimes he gets so angry with himself for me not understanding him.

I realize I was given a gift. Marc having autism is not just for me or just about me. Everything has a purpose and a reason. I know that I was given Marc for the building of the Kingdom of Christ. I must look beyond myself and my need to reason within my own narrow view of this world. I must stop trying to blame myself or someone else and just praise God for the gift of life He entrusted me with.

This gift, who I named Marc Antoni Brown, is continuing to take me through this journey and draw me closer to the purpose that God has ordained for me.

LESSON LEARNED:

Sometimes our blessings and our greatest gifts are in the imperfections.

SUCCESS

"Consider it nothing but joy, my brothers and sisters,
whenever you fall to various trials."

– James 1:2 AMP

Report cards came home today, and wow, I was amazed. My beautiful baby boy made honor roll!! Yes, he is considered to be "behind," but he does his work and made honor roll!! The best thing about it is he was happy. He understood what he had accomplished. He was proud of himself for his accomplishments in school.

"Marc, please get me your bag."

Marc ran and got his book bag out of his room and gave it to me. He didn't run away as he normally does, but he stood there next to me waiting. I opened his book bag, and he reached in and pulled out his daily communication book. He opened it for me and started pulling out the papers that were in front and handed them to me. This was new! Marc never pulled out papers for me or got so excited for me to see his communication book. I took the papers, and his eyes stayed glued to my face. As I looked at the row of B's with one A sandwiched in the middle, I began to smile. My baby had done it! His smile broke through at the same time as mine and he put his hand up for a high five.

"Way to go Marc! Mommy is so proud of you!" I said, as I gave him his high five.

"Do you want to show daddy?"

Marc took the report card and ran into the room to show his dad. I heard his dad say, "Good job Marc!"

I saw Marc with the biggest smile on his face, run out of the room with his dad as if he had just given him all the candy in the world. Marc gave me another high five and a hug and then went to the computer.

For the first time, Marc's Individual Education Plan (IEP) Progress Report read:

"Satisfactory progress towards meeting annual goals number one, two, three, four, five, six."

The comments section read:

"Marc is making progress on all IEP goals."

I was so afraid of him moving on to middle school. I remember walking into his new 6th grade classroom thinking this may be too much for him. I then started reading the teacher's daily lessons with goals and standards and thought "Wow! I don't know if Marc can handle this much structure." Well Marc laid all my concerns to rest. He can handle it and according to his teacher, he can handle even more.

Looking back, I believe that we as parents can sometimes hinder our own children. We want to protect them so much that we stop them from achieving what they can do. When I first met the teacher and saw the work expected of Marc, I thought this teacher was going to push Marc too hard. I just knew the teacher was going to have to change the expectations and demands. If not, I was going to have to change Marc's school. In my quest to help Marc succeed, I forgot that in order to succeed, we must have a task set in front of us, a challenge of sorts. Without that task, without that hill to climb, without that goal, there is no success. Without that unyielding fight to success, there is no learning, no growth, and no victory.

LESSON LEARNED:

Much the same way, God wants us to be victorious. How can we be victorious if we have nothing to have victory over? He wants to say well done, so that we can feel like that child whose dad just gave him a candy store!

Meanwhile, we want God to protect us from the task in front of us. We want God to take away the mountain that we must climb. But He wants us to know that we can only have success and victory when we conquer the task at hand, when we climb the mountain, or knock it down!

As we tackle that mountain and as we strive for those goals, our God is there rooting for us and He is ready to brush us off and encourage us if we fall. The same way we cheer our children on to triumph, God is cheering us on! At the end we will know that we have succeeded and feel the victory of being on "the honor roll.

COMPASSION

"Let all bitterness, and wrath, and anger, and clamor, and railing, be put away from you, with all malice; and be ye kind one to another, tenderhearted, forgiving each other, even as God also in Christ forgave you."

– Ephesians 4: 31-32 ASV

Kobe, the four-year-old, was upset because another child stuck her tongue out at him. His feelings were hurt, and he began to quietly cry. Marc was in another room, and he came out running towards Kobe. He bent down and looked closely at the tears falling from Kobe's eyes then looked up at me waiting for me to do something.

"Kobe what's wrong?" I asked.

"She stuck out her tongue at me."

"Who, Kobe?"

"The baby."

My friend was across the room holding her 13-month baby girl.

"Kobe, she didn't do that on purpose. Everything is okay. Please stop crying."

The entire time, Marc was bent down beside me, looking back and forth between Kobe and me as we had this conversation.

Kobe looked up at me. The tears continued to come down his eyes. "Kobe, please stop crying. She did not mean it. It's okay. Mommy needs you to be a big boy. She is just a baby. Can you please stop crying?"

Marc put his hand on Kobe's chest and began to rub the

front of his shirt. Then he gently moved his hand to Kobe's face and wiped the tears away. He leaned in and kissed him on the cheek and hugged him. Kobe stopped crying and looked at Marc. Marc moved in close to Kobe's face and just looked deeply into his eyes as if to make sure no tears were going to fall again.

"I wuv you Kobe-ya," Marc said and then rubbed his shirt again.

Kobe just looked at Marc. They stared at each other for a brief moment. It must have been some type of code between the two of them because when their eyes parted one another, Marc disappeared to the room he was playing in just as quickly as he had appeared. I just smiled. My child, the one with autism, showed me that he understood others' feelings and emotions. But bigger than that, he showed me he was sensitive to the needs of others and will stop what he is doing to run to their aid. He knew what it meant to be "thy brother's keeper" and knew his role.

LESSON LEARNED:

Often times in life, we forget about compassion. We forget that sometimes all it takes are the words: "I love you," or "I care about you." Sometimes we forget that we're not the only ones with feelings. Just like we need a hug, others need the same. We often desire to have someone wipe away our tears and then look deeply into our eyes and make sure we're okay. We long for someone to recognize our distinct cry from a distance, drop what they are doing, and come running to our aid.

Wow!

God just used my child! Yes, the one with autism, to show me how He works. To show me who He is. To show me how special I am to Him.

We all have a purpose in this life which God has

ordained. That includes my child with autism. I must let him live his purpose. I can't try and change it; I can't try and alter it; but I can learn from him and be blessed by watching him. I don't know what Marc's ultimate purpose is, but I know at this point in his life, his assignment was to show me the compassion of God. So, instead of me always telling him to go sit down when he rushes toward someone, or just thinking the negative when he does something out of the ordinary, I've decided to let him finish what he's been assigned to do. It has blessed me so.

A CHANGE IN ROUTINE

"Yet you do not know [the least thing] about what may happen in your life tomorrow. [What is secure in your life?] You are merely a vapor [like a puff of smoke or a wisp of steam from a cooking pot] that is visible for a little while and then vanishes [into thin air]."
– James 4:14 AMP

Marc likes routine. He knows what we do in the morning and the order in which we do it. I have learned that when it comes to my child with autism, having a daily routine is one of the most effective strategies to stop him from becoming frustrated or lashing out.

One summer Marc was attending summer camp. He loved it! This was his second year participating and he would get extremely excited when we pulled into the parking lot. Every morning he knew the routine. We dropped Kobe off at daycare, we took daddy to work, we would go down the same street to take him and Sean Jr. to camp, I would then take Tatiana to summer reading camp, and it ended with me going to school. This particular morning, I was running behind. I dropped Kobe off, then took his dad to work, but then I did something different. I did not go on the same street I usually went on every morning to take him and Sean Jr. to camp. Instead, I jumped on the Interstate to take Tatiana to school first. Marc was content in the back seat. He just stared out the window and rolled his paper in his hands. As I began to exit off the highway, Marc leaned forward toward the driver seat and said, "Where go-ing?"

Tatiana and Sean Jr. began to laugh. I said, "Marc, I have to take Tatiana to school. She is late."

He looked puzzled because I had used too many words in my explanation.

I clarified, "Tati school, then Marc camp."

Marc put a smile on his face and sat back to enjoy the ride. He said nothing else.

LESSON LEARNED:

Many times, I become comfortable in my routine. I do everything the same way because that is what works and that's what many of us are used to. The suddenly it seems like God decides to not drive us down the same street that we're used to going down. Things start coming at us so fast, as if we were driving 70 mph on the Interstate. We look up and wonder, "God where going?"

God replies, "You're going to the same place - your purpose. The final destination. But you can't get there quite yet. We must drop some other things off first: your attitude, your impatience, your selfishness, and your pride. So, I am gifting you with a child with autism to help you get to your destination whole, safe, and right with Me. So just sit back because you will get where you're going, and although you may think you are late, it will be right on time."

My advice: Sit back and enjoy the ride. Take in the scenery. Marc is still teaching me that it's OK to ask questions, but once I realize who's driving the car, I must rest.

I am not perfect, no human is, but God has given me Marc to help teach me, guide me, and lead me closer to that place of perfection in Him. Just as Marc trusted me, I must trust the driver of my life knowing that He will get me where He wants me to be.

BROTHERLY LOVE

"Jesus said to the father, 'Why did you say 'if you can'? All things are possible for the one who believes."
— Mark 9:23 ERV

"Always be full of joy. Never stop praying. Whatever happens, always be thankful. This is how God wants you to live in Christ Jesus."
— 1 Thessalonians 5: 16-18 ERV

"Seek the Lord and His strength; Seek His face continually [longing to be in His presence].
— 1 Chronicles 16: 11 AMP

Many times, when people talk about children with autism, they talk about the social withdrawal. That is actually one of the first questions the doctor asked me. "How does he get along with other children? How does he get along with his siblings? Does he have any interactions with other children, or does he just stay to himself?"

I recall when Marc was first diagnosed, at the age of 2 1/2 years old, the answer to the questions were: "He doesn't really play with other children. He is usually by himself. He really doesn't interact much with his older brother. He is tremendously upset if his brother takes something he has been playing with."

What a difference prayer, time, love, hope, and patience made in Marc's life.

I recall when Marc and his baby brother Kobe, who was 3 years old, started running through the house. My first instinct was to tell them to stop running before someone got hurt. I looked up and said, "Guys, stop the running because..."

"No Honey don't stop them, they're playing," my husband interrupted. "They're playing with each other. Watch."

I stopped and gave them my full attention.

Marc would dash by me and run to his room. Kobe would soon follow with his arms in the air, hands curled like claws, growling. Marc would begin to giggle, the closer Kobe got to him. Then he would dart to the side so Kobe would not catch him and run the other way laughing. After a few times, something on television got Kobe's attention, so he stopped to watch. Marc was not ready to stop. He walked up to Kobe and said, "MUNSTUR" in a deep voice imitating a monster. Kobe looked up and smiled at Marc and quickly put his claws back over his head. Marc took off running and laughing, not to let the monster get him.

At one point Kobe ran to his room and closed and locked the door. Marc knocked on the door. Kobe started growling by the door. Marc said, "Open dee dora, open dee dora! Kobe dash-uh, open dee dora!"

I went over to the door and tried to open it and realized Kobe had locked it. I said, "Kobe, open the door! No locked doors in the house."

Kobe opened the door, and Marc took off running. Kobe looked up at me and said, "Mommy, but the monster needed a break!"

After a while they both settled down on their own. They sat on the carpet in the living room side by side. Then Kobe stood up, Marc turned to look at Kobe trying to figure out what Kobe was going to do. Kobe walked in front of Marc. Marc got up and knelt on his knees in front of Kobe. Then Marc reached out his arms to hug his baby brother!

Kobe walked into Marc's arms and Marc pretended that it knocked him backwards so back they both went. Marc never let go of his brother. He was determined that Kobe would not get hurt in the short fall to the carpet. Marc made sure that Kobe fell on top of him and then he gently rolled him onto the carpet. Of course, boys being boys, this began a new game for the two of them.

Marc got up on his knees and Kobe faced Marc. Kobe took a couple of steps back and waited for Marc to hold out his arms. Kobe ran. Marc caught him in his arms, wrapped his arms around him, and fell sideways making Kobe believe he was tackling him. Marc and Kobe were both laughing. Kobe said, "Marc, Marc, watch this. I'ma use a new move on ya!"

This time Marc responded with a huge smile and got into position with his arms outstretched. Then the wrestling match would begin again. I looked over at my husband, who was sitting near them in the living room, and what I saw will forever be etched in my head. I saw a proud father looking at his son with the biggest smile on his face. He looked up at me and said, "What?" questioning me looking at him. I didn't have to explain my look. He then explained, "I like to see Marc and Kobe play with one another."

I said, "I know, this is a proud daddy moment!"

He shook his head in agreement and began to referee the match.

LESSON LEARNED:

Don't always believe what you read and even what you might be going through at the moment. Continue to have hope. Continue to be determined. Look at each little thing as an accomplishment. Marc may not be walking around the house using his verbal skills like my other three children, but I knew that it was there. I needed to stop viewing things as negative. So what, my child has autism and wants to be alone? Sometimes, I want to be alone. Sometimes I know I don't want to be bothered and playing with others. There is nothing wrong with that. I just cherish the moments Marc doesn't want to be alone. Whether it's a moment when he comes and wants a hug, he just wants me to apply pressure as only I can, or if it's a moment he needs help with something. I cherish it!

I don't fill journals with pages of what Marc did not accomplish. I fill journals with pages of what he did accomplish.

A life lesson that I have learned from this experience is: With prayer, time, love, hope, determination, will and patience ALL THINGS ARE POSSIBLE!

THEIR FUTURES ARE BRIGHT

"The one who guards his mouth [thinking before he speaks] protects his life; The one who opens his lips wide [and chatters without thinking] comes to ruin."
— Proverbs 13:3 AMP

"A soothing tongue [speaking words that build up and encourage] is a tree of life, but a perversive tongue [speaking words that overwhelm and depress] crushes the spirit."
— Proverbs 15:4 AMP

Someone once said to me, "so you know you will have Marc with you for the rest of your life?"

I wondered if they were for real! I responded, "Why do you say that?"

"Because you know... his condition."

"What condition?"

"His autism."

"OK, what about his autism?"

They looked puzzled as if they were trying to find a polite way to explain something without breaking my heart. "Well, you know he is going to depend on you?"

I replied, "All of my children depend on me, and will depend on me to be their mother as long as I am alive."

"But, you know, he needs more help!"

I know as parents of children on the autism spectrum, we can find ourselves in this type of conversation. Or we have this conversation with ourselves a lot. Why? Really, why do we do this? What stops a child that was diagnosed with autism from having hopes and dreams? What stops them from living on their own? What stops them from taking care of themselves in some way? Why do others believe that they can't? Yes, I know that there are some children that will have to totally depend on their parents or caregiver(s) to supply their daily needs, but why is it always assumed of all? Yes, I do know that Marc may have to be with me, but why does everyone assume that?

News flash:

My child may not be "normal." That's because my child, whether we say my autistic child or my child with autism, nonetheless MY child is greater than normal! He can remember the most complex tasks. He can achieve things beyond my understanding. He can organize, build, and create things that others cannot even imagine. He has a pure heart and pure intentions. He is creative, innovative, determined, and one of a kind. He can do for himself if I teach him and if I allow him.

So how did I respond to that person who believed that without a shadow of a doubt, without getting to know the abilities of my child? I said, "Marc will grow up. Marc will graduate high school. Marc may or may not go to college. Marc will get some type of job. Marc may or may not get married and have kids of his own. But understand this, that's how it works for every child, not just Marc. Marc can clothe himself, brush his teeth, bathe himself, get food out of the refrigerator when he is hungry, ask me to get him juice when he is thirsty, picks out food at the grocery store, and knows what he likes and dislikes. So, I know Marc will be OK."

"What if that doesn't happen?" they replied.

My answer to them and to anyone who wants to ask the same question is: "I don't choose to live my life around what ifs. Life and death are in the power of the tongue, and I choose life. So, I speak life."

LESSON LEARNED:

Life is full of what ifs. I have learned to trust and have faith in God because Marc could wake up tomorrow talking in full sentences and doing everything on his own. With God all things are possible.

> *"But even if He does not, let it be known to you, O king, that we are not going to serve your gods or worship the golden image that you have set up!" Daniel 3: 18 AMP*

SLOWING IT DOWN

"If anyone has ears to hear, let him hear."
— Mark 7:16 AMP

"Don't be pulled in different directions or worried about a thing. Be saturated in prayer throughout each day, offering your faith-filled requests before God with overflowing gratitude. Tell him every detail of your life, then God's wonderful peace that transcends human understanding, will guard your heart and mind through Jesus Chris."
— Philippians 4:6-7 TPT

Marc was sitting at the table eating. In the middle of him eating, he got up from the table and walked over to his dad. "DADDEEISPIDAGASS."

His dad looked at him with wide eyes. "What Marc?"

"DADDEEISPIDAGASS."

"OK, Marc. I need you to slow down. Say it again."

"DADDYEESPIDAGASS."

His dad thought about it and began to repeat him slowly, "D-A- D- D- Y- I- S- P- I- D- A- G- A- S-S."

His dad repeated it again, a little faster. "Daddy I spid a glass."

Then he got it! "Marc, you spilled a glass?"

Marc smiled and said, "IWIPEITUH" and showed his dad the towel he used to wipe up the juice that had spilled.

His dad ran into the room to tell me. We were both so excited that Marc used a full sentence and initiated a conversation. Also, Marc knew what he was supposed to do, and he did it on his own.

I went to Marc's open house at school and was sharing this accomplishment with his teacher and a parent that knew Marc from his previous school. I began talking about how Marc puts all his words together and talks very fast and how important it is to be patient to try and figure out what he is saying. I explained how sometimes I just had to say it slower.

At that point the parents said, "Well, you do know you talk extremely fast too? He's talking just like you."

I began to think back to when I first tried to help Marc pronounce words after his diagnosis. I used to talk extremely slow to make sure I pronounced every letter in the word. The result was Marc saying, "DOGUH" instead of "DOG."

Now his vocabulary has slightly enhanced, he listens to how he is supposed to talk, and he mimics. Who did he choose to listen to and mimic? Yes, me! His dad has a drawn-out southern drawl that I guess Marc thought was a little too slow, so he chose the other extreme.

As I write this I chuckle. Marc and I had a conversation this morning. My oldest son interrupted us and said, "Can you both slow down? I don't know what either of you are saying!"

The funny thing was I understood Marc and Marc understood me. So, should I be accompanying him to the speech therapist? Do I need some work too?

LESSON LEARNED:

To hear what they hear! To see what they see! What was said to be babbling and gibberish was actually a language that we could understand. I always thought he was really speaking another language, but I just needed to listen more intently and say the words slower.

It's funny, to figure out that the other language, the babble and the gibberish, is Marc mimicking what I sound like to him. He is speaking English, the same language I am speaking.

So, God, I got your message loud and clear today: SLOW DOWN, PATRICE!

Not just in talking but in all things, I must take my time and slow my roll.

THE JOURNEY

"For as the heavens are high above the earth, so great is his lovingkindness toward those who fear and worship Him [with awe-filled respect and deepest reverence]. As far as the east from the west, So far has He removed our transgressions from us. Just as a father loves his children, So the Lord loves those who fear and worship Him [with awe-filled respect and deepest reverence]."

– Psalms 103: 11-13 AMP

I don't want to fool anyone into thinking that as challenges came up with Marc and continue to come up with Marc, I just look to the Lord and have the answer. That is not how it works at all. Challenges came and may continue to come; some I will pass and others I will fail.

Marc would sometimes start screaming in a high pitch voice in the middle of the store and I didn't know what to do. I didn't look to God for help. Like a typical parent would, I looked him dead in the eye, and had a few stern words with him.

I remember one time while at church, Marc decided to fall out in the middle of the floor and scream loudly while kicking and flailing his hands. Without thinking, I reached down to the floor and pulled him back up to his feet by his collar. I looked at him in the eye and said "You will not fall out! Do you hear me? Mommy does not do that!" He looked stunned and then turned and walked away quietly.

In the midst of that, I did not see that God was

preparing me to change my career to become a teacher with classes of students that had various learning abilities and learning styles. He was building patience, gentleness, humbleness, and mercy up in me by allowing me to raise Marc. Of course, hindsight is 20/20 because what I saw was my child testing and trying me.

Another time, when Marc was trying to tell me what he wanted and I didn't understand, he started yelling and screaming in a high pitch shrill. I started yelling and screaming with him, making the same noises. I just didn't know what to do. We did this together for 5 to 10 minutes. We did it until I got tired. I finally stopped and told him to just go to his room. He was so upset that he started throwing things and hitting things. I didn't understand that Marc was desperately trying to communicate with me. I saw it as him just screaming and throwing a tantrum so, in my helplessness, I threw my own temper tantrum along with him.

There are many more times that I can recall. The list goes on and on. Those were the times that, had I just stopped from my schedule, stopped thinking about myself, and just calmed down patiently without responding out of emotions, I would have not reacted the way I did.

LESSON LEARNED:

I may not get it right the first time or the second time, but because of my desire and love for Marc, I will keep trying. If I take that love and multiply it by infinity, that is God's love for me. Although I mess up time and time again, He still loves me enough to give me a gift named Marc to make me better.

For God so [greatly] loved and dearly prized the world, that He [even] gave His [One and] only begotten Son, so that whoever believes and trusts in Him [as Savior] shall not perish but have eternal life. For God did not send the Son into the world to judge and condemn the world [that is, to initiate final judgement of the world], but that the world might be saved through Him. Whoever believes and has decided to trust in Him [as personal Savior and Lord] is not judged [for this one, there is no judgment, no rejection, no condemnation]; but the one who does not believe [and has decided to reject Him as personal Savior and Lord] is judged already [that one has been convicted and sentenced], because he has not believed and trusted in the name of the [One and] only begotten Son of God [the One who Is truly unique, the only One of His kind, the One who alone can save him].

– John 3:16-18 AMP